21st Century Skills INNOVATION Library

From Cats' Eyes to . . . Reflectors

by Wil Mara

Published in the United States of America by Cherry Lake Publishing
Ann Arbor, Michigan
www.cherrylakepublishing.com

Content Adviser: Robert Friedel, PhD, Professor of History, University of Maryland, College Park, Maryland

Design: The Design Lab

Photo Credits: Cover and page 3, ©Dariush M./Shutterstock, Inc.; cover (inset), ©Grietpear/Dreamstime.com; page 4, ©Jeffrey Van Daele/Shutterstock, Inc.; page 5, ©Igumnova Irina/Shutterstock, Inc.; page 7, ©Witr/Dreamstime.com; page 9, ©The Print Collector/Alamy; page 10, ©Timbooth2770/Dreamstime.com; page 11, ©Tomd/Dreamstime.com; page 13, ©Martin Harvey/Alamy; page 14, ©Richard Zanettacci/Alamy; page 15, ©Mark Bourdillon/Alamy; page 16, ©Nicola Vernizzi/Dreamstime.com; page 17, ©AfriPics.com/Alamy; page 19, ©Lorenz Britt/Alamy; page 20, ©Tony Strong/Shutterstock, Inc.; page 21, ©SuperStock/Alamy; page 23, ©Vereshchagin Dmitry/Shutterstock, Inc.; page 25, ©Richard Sheppard/Alamy; page 26, ©Alexander Chaikin/Shutterstock, Inc.; page 27, ©Four Oaks/Shutterstock, Inc.; page 29, ©svetlana55/Shutterstock, Inc.

Library of Congress Cataloging-in-Publication Data
Mara, Wil.
From cats' eyes to . . . reflectors / by Wil Mara.
p. cm.–(Innovations from nature)
Includes bibliographical references and index.
Audience: 4 to 6.
ISBN 978-1-61080-500-1 (lib. bdg.) – ISBN 978-1-61080-587-2 (e-book) –
ISBN 978-1-61080-674-9 (pbk.)
1. Biomimicry–Juvenile literature. 2. Reflectors (Safety devices)–Juvenile literature. I. Title.
T173.8.M3585 2013
681'.4–dc23 2012008672

Cherry Lake Publishing would like to acknowledge the work of The Partnership for 21st Century Skills. Please visit www.21stcenturyskills.org *for more information.*

Printed in the United States of America
Corporate Graphics Inc.
July 2012
CLFA11

CONTENTS

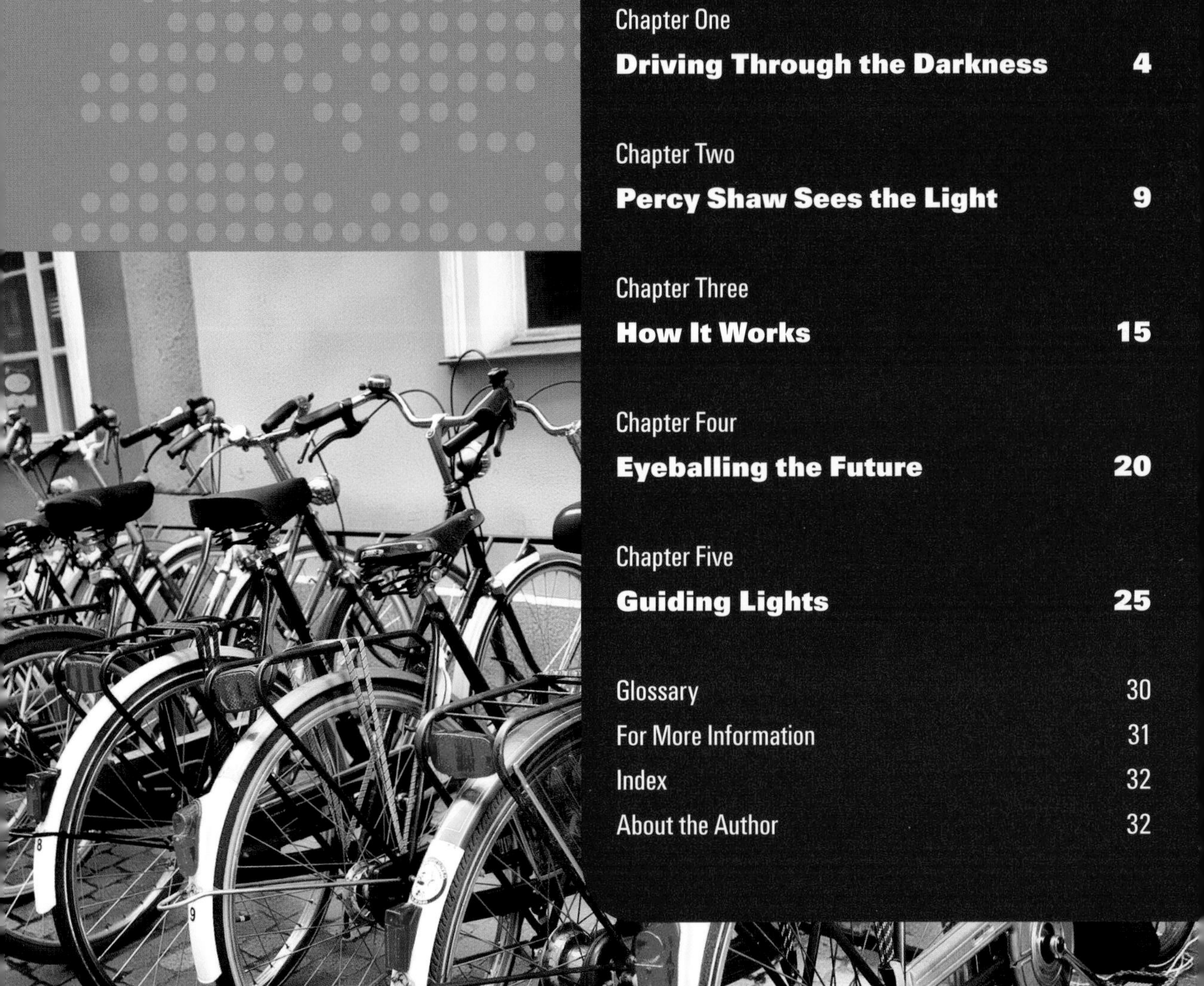

CHAPTER ONE

Driving Through the Darkness

Driving in poor weather conditions or at night make it very difficult to see.

Have you ever been on a dark road in the dead of night? A road that had no lighting at all? On the darkest of nights, when there's no moon in the sky, cruising down the road can be very dangerous. Suppose the road suddenly takes a sharp turn, and the driver doesn't notice until the last second? He may not have enough time to react and keep his car on the roadway. Poor weather conditions, such as rain, snow, or fog, would make such a journey down a dark road even more dangerous.

In addition to reducing visibility, snowstorms make it difficult for drivers to control their vehicles.

Learning & Innovation Skills

Road safety has come a long way since the early days of the gas-powered vehicle. Countless safety features and improved signage on today's highways and byways have replaced yesterday's rough road surfaces and lack of signs or markings. Many roads now have a series of grooves, called rumble strips, cut into the **shoulder** of the road. When a car's tires run over the strips, they make a loud noise, instantly alerting the driver that he or she has drifted too far out of the lane. Modern highway signs are large and easy to read, even at night. Some electronic signs can tell drivers about the road conditions ahead and provide an estimated time of arrival to points farther down the road.

The earliest roads were very different from today's modern roads that are made with smooth **pavement**. They were simple dirt pathways worn into the ground from constant use by people and animals. Roads paved with bricks were used in cities that flourished in India as early as 3250 to 2750 BCE. Ancient Egypt's earliest roads were probably built about 2600 BCE. They were constructed to provide a solid roadway for transporting the enormous blocks of stone used to build the pyramids. The ancient Romans laid thousands of miles of stone-covered roadways for use by their armies. Some of these early Roman roads were so well constructed that they are still in use today!

The ancient Romans and Greeks were the first to put lights on their roadways. The earliest streetlamps were fueled by oil. People who lived near the roads, often slaves, lit the lamps

Early roads were not smooth, and only a few were lit, like those we are used to having today.

every evening. By the middle of the 19th century, gas-powered streetlights were common throughout Europe and the United States. By the end of the century, they were replaced by electric lights. But even as these became more common, there were still long stretches of road that had no lighting at all. Building, powering, and maintaining streetlights were all very expensive, so lights were more common in busy city areas than the more open and undeveloped lands outside the cities. As a result, it was often risky to travel on country roads after sundown.

As motorized vehicles became more widely used in the early 20th century, accidents in these unlit outlying areas became common. Although electric headlights had been in use by 1898, an additional safety feature was needed to provide nighttime motorists with a way of safely navigating through the darkness. Amazingly, a simple solution was found in a most unexpected place—the animal kingdom.

CHAPTER TWO

Percy Shaw Sees the Light

Percy Shaw was born in England in 1890. Even as a child, he was an original and independent thinker with a very inventive mind. His father worked in a cloth mill, and by the time Percy was 13, he had left school and taken a job at the mill as an **apprentice**. He soon grew tired of the long hours and low pay, and moved on to a series of positions in various engineering companies.

World War I forced many areas to observe "blackout conditions" where streetlights had to be turned off during the night.

When World War I (1914–1918) began, his father

started a weapons manufacturing business. Percy joined his father's company as a junior partner. When his father passed away in 1929, Percy went into a new profession, building and maintaining roadways. In his spare time, he tinkered with cars and motorcycles. His mechanical experience positioned him perfectly to be the creator of an invention that would soon change the world.

After work one evening in the early 1930s, Shaw dropped in at a local pub to relax. Driving home, he encountered several hazardous road conditions. It was dark and foggy, and there were no streetlamps to light

Fog adds to the hazards of nighttime driving.

Streetlights make it much easier for drivers to see at night.

21st Century Content

At first, Percy Shaw's roadstud idea was not met with much enthusiasm. The English government had to give its approval for the roadstuds to be used throughout England. Government officials, however, were not eager to invest large sums of money to have the roadstuds manufactured and installed along thousands of miles of roadway. At the time that Shaw received a **patent** for his invention in 1934, he was unable to convince the government to undertake the project. But when World War II (1939–1945) began and German planes started nighttime bombing raids on England, the country was forced into blackout conditions. Streetlights and lights on vehicles had to be turned off at night to make it difficult for enemy planes to find their targets. Under these circumstances, the English government asked Shaw to produce as many roadstuds as possible. Shaw went on to become a very wealthy man—and demonstrated the importance of sticking with an idea when you know it's the right one!

the roadway. Also, the shiny, steel streetcar rails that were built into the roadway had recently been removed because the streetcar that used them had been taken out of service. In the past, even on the most treacherous nights, drivers could rely on the reflection of these rails to guide them.

Shaw was very nervous and afraid that he might swerve off the road. No one is certain exactly what happened next, because many different versions of Shaw's story have been told through the years. The one that might best explain his invention, however, is that his car's headlights passed over the eyes of a stray cat. The light that reflected back gave Shaw his groundbreaking idea.

That idea became the inspiration for a device that Shaw would spend the rest of his life developing, manufacturing, and improving: the Catseye reflecting

Have you ever seen a cat's eyes glowing at night?

roadstud. It consisted of a pair of reflecting glass "eyes" set into a little dome made of tough but flexible rubber, which was then surrounded by an iron housing for protection. These early roadstuds were put into the middle of a road at regular intervals. Even though the top of the rubber dome was left uncovered, the iron housing that surrounded it was high enough so that a car's tires would not damage the dome. The edges of the iron housing were also slanted upward so that car tires would roll up and over the roadstud. Because of this durable construction, one Catseye roadstud could provide safe guidance to motorists for many years.

Cars can easily drive over the tops of Catseye roadstuds without damaging them.

CHAPTER THREE

How It Works

Percy Shaw's invention was based on the concept of **biomimicry**. Simply put, biomimicry is the practice of copying nature—plants and animals—to build or improve something. Shaw's roadstud was not the first device inspired by nature, and it surely won't be the last. In fact, biomimicry is a rapidly emerging field in scientific research.

Percy Shaw's invention has no doubt saved countless lives.

The roadstud's properties are similar to those of cats' eyes. Cats have a layer of tissue at the back of their eyes known as a **tapetum lucidum**. This is a Latin phrase that means "bright tapestry." The tapetum lucidum reflects light that enters the cat's eye. In doing so, it creates more light for a cat to use when it's trying to see. Cats are able to see well in the dark: their eyes absorb all

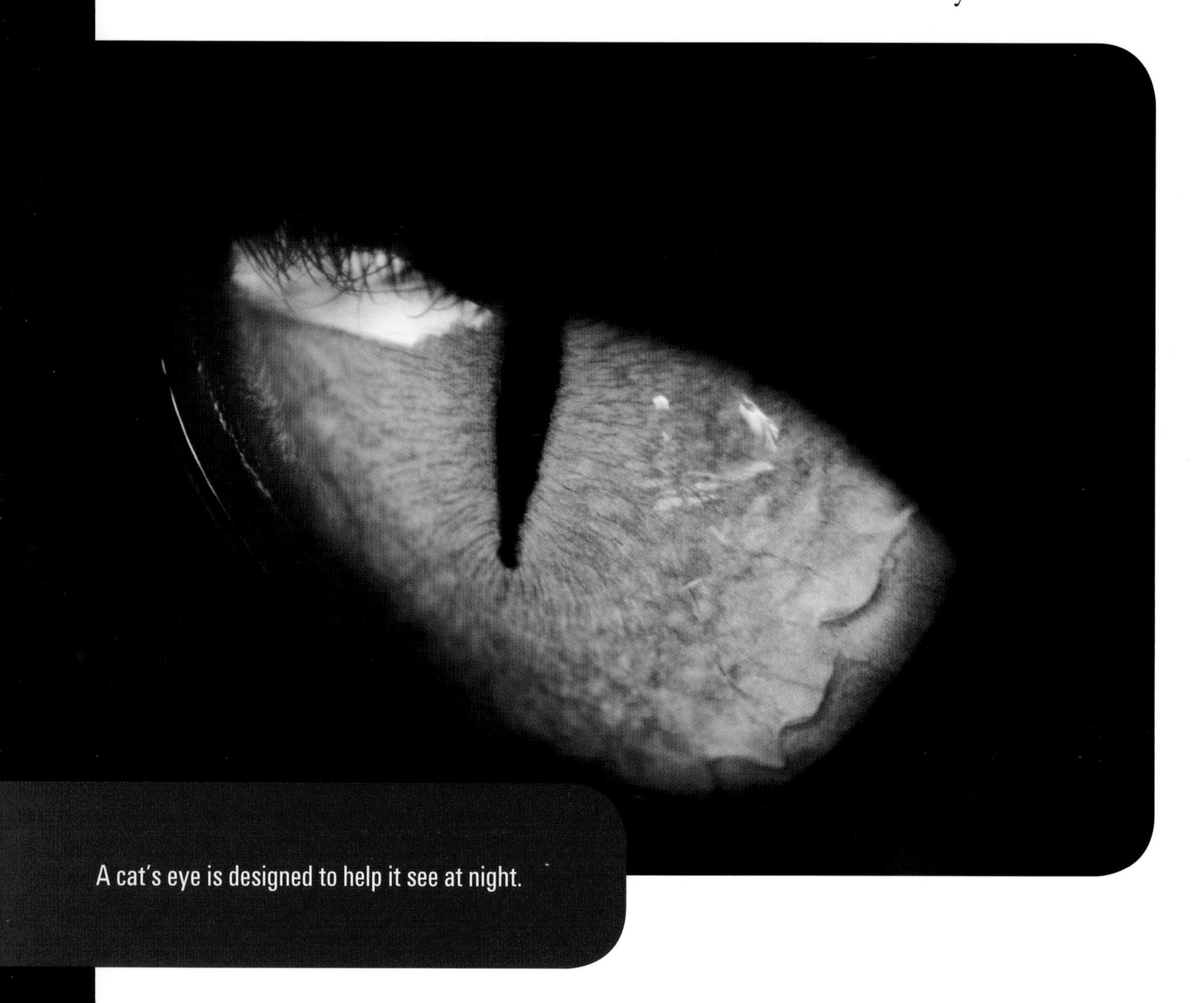

A cat's eye is designed to help it see at night.

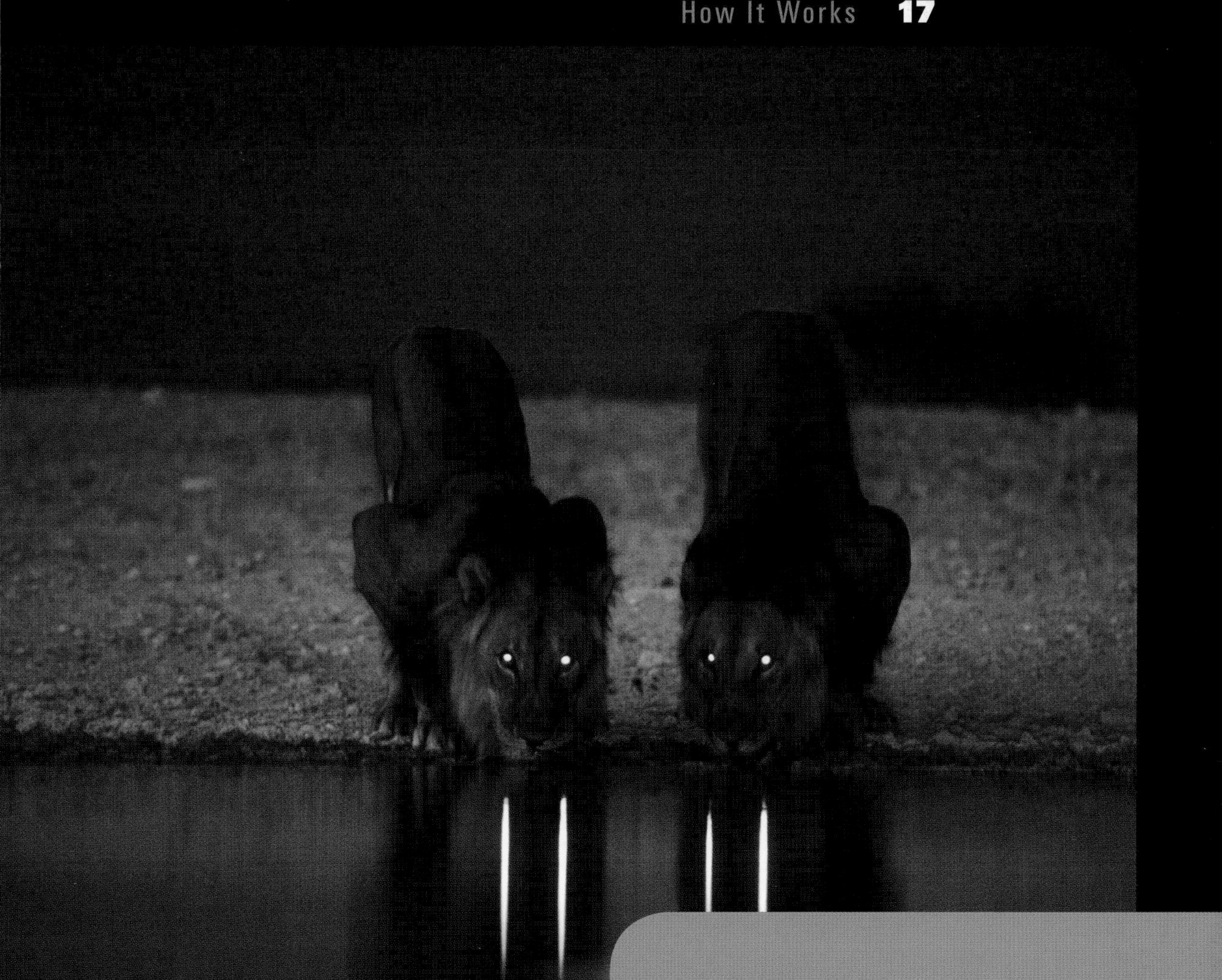

Eyeshine occurs in animals of all kinds.

of the available light and then send it back out. This is also why cats' eyes have a reflective, mirrorlike quality. This characteristic is called **eyeshine**. Dogs, raccoons, cows, sheep, many fish, and a variety of birds also have a tapetum lucidum.

21st Century Content

Percy Shaw may have invented the roadstud, but he did not invent the small reflective "eye" that was based on the eyes of a cat. Reflectors were probably in use during the 1920s, years before his roadstud idea. Richard Hollins Murray, an English accountant, patented ways to fix reflectors to a surface and to protect them from damage seven years before Shaw patented his roadstud. Shaw acknowledged Murray as an important contributor to the development of roadstuds, and he offered Murray a percentage of the profits he made. Murray declined this generous offer but still made a place for himself in history.

The "eyes" in Percy Shaw's roadstuds were small bodies of glass shaped like little bullets. They had a rounded front and a reflective, mirrorlike coating at the back. The rubber dome that held them featured a "wiping action" that cleaned off the front of the eyes every time a car ran over them. Shaw eventually designed a double-sided roadstud that had eyes on both sides, providing guidance to drivers coming from both directions.

In time, different reflector colors were used for different purposes and placement. White reflectors were placed in the center of a road, red were placed along the shoulder, yellow along a raised **median**, and so on. Eventually, roadstuds became so popular that Shaw began manufacturing them for countries throughout the world.

In difficult driving conditions, reflectors are critical to helping drivers get through dangerous curves.

CHAPTER FOUR

Eyeballing the Future

Percy Shaw's original design has inspired the development of many other types of reflecting roadstuds.

Percy Shaw's Catseye reflecting roadstud has undergone numerous improvements since he first began producing it. Other devices based on his concept have been designed to serve a similar purpose.

The raised pavement marker is usually a piece of rectangular plastic with slanted ramps on two sides so a car's tires can easily roll over them. The slanted ramps hold the plastic

Some road markers have a curved shape.

reflective material in place. The markers are set directly into the road surface like the roadstuds. They are less expensive to produce than roadstuds since there is no metal or glass involved, but they are also less durable and occasionally separate from the road surface.

Learning & Innovation Skills

How cool would it be to make yourself invisible? Although the technology to do this does not yet exist, someday it might, thanks to a natural element known as reflectin. Reflectin is a protein found in certain squids in the Pacific Ocean. It has many interesting properties, including a tendency to be highly reflective. Some scientists believe reflectin could be used to create a thin film that reflects light in such a way that the film would not be visible from certain angles. Even in its early stage of development, reflectin research may bring us one step closer to turning Harry Potter's famous invisibility cloak into a reality.

Similar to these are flexible traffic pillars, which appear like "sticks" coming up out of the road, often with a reflective lens perched at the top. These have proven particularly useful for guiding drivers through construction areas where the flow of traffic moves away from its normal course. Often they are attached to springs or pivots at their base, allowing them to bend and snap back to their upright position if struck by a vehicle.

One variation to Shaw's Catseye roadstud that has not yet proven totally successful has been the flashing-light stud. These were made to blink so rapidly that a driver only "sensed" the flash and got a feeling of urgency (in case, for example, there was an accident or other hazard ahead). These devices, however, had several drawbacks. The flash distracted some drivers, drawing their attention away from the road. Also, the rapid flashing may possibly trigger violent episodes in

As reflector technology continues to improve, more car crashes can be prevented.

drivers who suffer from **epilepsy**, a disorder of the nervous system that can result in convulsions and loss of consciousness. Researchers are currently working on new technology to solve the disadvantages of flashing-light studs.

Retroreflective material, or material that reflects light, is another new useful technology and is becoming commonly used on clothing. Drivers can more easily see people walking or jogging in reflective clothing. Bike riders often attach reflective pads to their bicycles for the same reason.

Inspired by the reflective quality of cats' eyes, some carmakers created vehicles with headlights that are set into mirror-backed housings. These not only increase each light's intensity but also provide reflected light to passing drivers in the event that a headlight blows out.

There are even reflective surfaces on movie screens, increasing the brilliance of the images to compensate for the darkness in the theater. It's amazing how many uses have been found for light-reflecting material and how many more are likely to be discovered in the future.

CHAPTER FIVE

Guiding Lights

Many creative thinkers have made important contributions to the worlds of both traffic safety and biomimicry. Here are just a few noteworthy innovators.

The Catseye roadstud is an amazing example of biomimicry at work.

Percy Shaw (1890–1976) was born and raised in England at a time when motorized vehicles were a new phenomenon. He took the chance on his roadstud invention, patented it,

Robert Full developed a wall-climbing machine after studying the way geckos scurry up vertical surfaces.

Robert Full also studied cockroaches when designing his wall-climbing machine.

invested time and money to produce it, and then worked tirelessly to have it accepted. For his lifesaving invention, Shaw was awarded the Order of the British Empire by the queen of England. He was always grateful for his good fortune and did not hesitate to help and encourage other people, including young inventors.

Robert Full is a biologist at the University of California at Berkeley who has carefully studied the movement of insects. He observed how a cockroach's legs allow it to run

Life & Career Skills

Technologies based on biomimicry are going to play an important role in the future. Many will be eco-friendly and do little or no harm to the natural world while providing benefits to people everywhere. If you're interested in "going green" as a career, focus on the natural sciences, and then consider a field where you can put your talent and experience to good use. Professional areas where you might one day seek employment include environmental research, teaching, engineering, and some areas of medicine.

at full speed across mesh surfaces and how a gecko's feet, with millions of tiny bristles, enables it to run straight up walls. Using his research, Full designed the robotic "distributed foot," adding spines and hairs to metal legs to create extremely mobile, scampering machines. Full helped create Spinybot, a robot that can walk up walls and glass like a gecko, and he's even helped create realistic insect animations for a major Hollywood film.

George de Mestral (1907–1990) is the inventor of Velcro. After returning home from a trip with his dog in the woods outside of Geneva, Switzerland, in 1941, de Mestral noticed that the burrs, or seeds, from a native plant kept sticking to his clothes and his dog's fur. He examined the burrs under a microscope and noticed that they had hundreds of tiny "hooks," which caught on anything with a loop, such as clothing, hair, or fur. De Mestral quickly began work to invent a system of binding two materials

Velcro has become one of the world's most commonly used fasteners.

together that could be used repeatedly. After years of experimentation, he was granted a patent in 1955 and opened shops around the world that manufactured his brilliant nature-inspired invention. De Mestral called his system Velcro—from the French words *velours* ("velvet") and *crochet* ("hook")—and today, it's one of the world's most widely used fasteners.

Glossary

apprentice (uh-PREN-tiss) someone who learns a trade or craft by working with a skilled person

biomimicry (bye-oh-MI-mi-kree) the practice of copying nature in order to build or improve something

epilepsy (EP-uh-lep-see) a disease of the brain that causes a person to have sudden blackouts or convulsions

eyeshine (EYE-shine) a glow of reflected light that appears in the eyes of animals

median (MEE-dee-uhn) a strip of land or a wall-like barrier dividing two or more lanes of traffic going in opposite directions

patent (PAT-int) a legal document giving the inventor of an item sole rights to manufacture or sell the item

pavement (PAYV-muhnt) a hard material, such as concrete or asphalt, that is used to cover roads or sidewalks

retroreflective (reh-troh-ree-FLEK-tiv) the ability to reflect light back to its source

shoulder (SHOHL-dur) the sloping side or edge of a road or highway

tapetum lucidum (tah-PEE-tum LOO-sih-dum) a layer of tissue at the back of some animals' eyes that reflects light

For More Information

BOOKS

Gates, Phil. *Nature Got There First.* New York: Kingfisher Publishing, 2010.

Lee, Dora. *Biomimicry.* Tonawanda, NY: Kids Can Press, 2011.

WEB SITES

Ask Nature—What Is Biomimicry?
www.asknature.org/article/view/what_is_biomimicry
Find out more about biomimicry, with examples, further links, and interesting video content.

Biomimlcry Institute and Biomimicry Guild
www.biomimicry.net
Check out the latest news on the science of biomimicry, with links to other sites as well as information for those interested in choosing a career in the field.

Reflecting Roadstuds Ltd.
www.percyshawcatseyes.com/index.php
Check out this site dedicated to Percy Shaw's invention of the Catseye reflecting roadstud. It features biographical information, the story of the roadstud's invention, technical information, and some links.

Index

About the Author

Wil Mara is the award-winning author of more than 120 books, many of which are educational titles for young readers. More information about his work can be found at www.wilmara.com.